D1423251

PADRE PIO

PADRE PIO

In My Own Words

Compiled and edited by
Anthony F. Chiffolo

Hodder & Stoughton
LONDON SYDNEY AUCKLAND

Compilation copyright © 2001 Anthony F. Chiffolo

The right of Anthony F. Chiffolo to be identified
as the Compiler of the Work has been asserted by
him in accordance with the Copyright, Designs
and Patents Act 1988.

First published in Great Britain in 2001 by
arrangement with Liguori Publications, Liguori,
Missouri, USA.

10 9 8 7 6 5 4 3 2 1

British Library Cataloguing in Publication Data
A record for this book is available from the British Library

ISBN 0 340 78557 8

Printed and bound in Great Britain by
Clays Ltd, St Ives plc

Hodder and Stoughton
A Division of Hodder Headline Ltd
338 Euston Road
London NW1 3BH

*May Jesus be pleased to instill
a little comfort in your hearts through
these poor words of mine.*

LETTER TO THE FIORENTINO SISTERS,
OCTOBER 30, 1916

———————————

*We are by Divine Grace,
at the dawn of a new year.
Since only God knows
whether we will finish this year,
we should spend it in reparation
for the past,
in preparation for the future;
good works go hand in hand
with good intentions.*

TIME OF BIRTH

Contents

INTRODUCTION

Many people believe Padre Pio to have been the greatest person of the last century, and he is often called "the second Saint Francis." He is one of the Church's most recently beatified, honored as "blessed" on May 2, 1999. Though he led a simple, holy life in the rugged mountains of southern Italy, he became a world-famous celebrity, and his fame sparked controversy and difficulties that retarded the promotion of his cause for canonization until long after his death.

Padre Pio was born Francesco Forgione on May 25, 1887, in Pietrelcina, a poor village inland from Naples, Italy. He was the fourth of six children, and his parents, Zi'Orazio and Giuseppa, were farmers who raised him and his siblings to be devout Roman Catholics.

From his earliest days Francesco showed a strong spiritual disposition, received visits from our Lady, and had various mystical experiences. He also knew that he was called to be a priest. He was accepted into the Capuchin Franciscan novitiate at the age of sixteen and took the name *Pio*, which means "pious." However, Pio became so weak with lung and intestinal troubles while in the seminary that he had to continue his studies at home, where his health showed some improvement. He remained in Pietrelcina for seven more years, studying, praying, fasting, suffering, and was dispensed for early ordination, receiving holy orders on August 10, 1910, at the age of twenty-three.

About a month later, on September 7, while Pio was praying in the reed hut he had built in his family's fields, Christ and Mary appeared before him, and Pio received the stigmata, Christ's wounds, in his own flesh. The stigmata were a great source of pain and also of embarrassment for Pio, but his only prayer was for the wounds to become invisible—and the Lord granted this prayer, for the time being.

During World War I, Pio was drafted into the army, but his health was still poor, and he was granted several periods of sick leave before he was finally discharged. Concurrently, Pio was moving back and forth between various monasteries and his hometown because he would become severely ill after only a short time in any cloister. His superiors finally allowed him to go to Our Lady of Grace Monastery at San Giovanni Rotondo in 1916, which at that time was a primitive and almost inaccessible place. The people of Pietrelcina were angry that Pio's superiors had "stolen" their hometown "saint," but Pio liked his new home, and his health eventually improved.

While hearing the boys' confessions at Our Lady of Grace on August 5, 1918, Pio received a vision in which a "celestial person" hurled a weapon into his soul; upon coming to himself, Pio realized that he had indeed been wounded physically and was bleeding from his side. This wound was eventually recognized as a transverberation of the heart.

A short few weeks later, on September 20, 1918, Pio was praying before the crucifix in the monastery chapel after Mass when he received another celestial visitor. From that moment until just before his death fifty years later, Pio bore the visible, bleeding wounds of Christ in his hands, feet, and side.

Pio wore half-gloves to hide the holes in his hands and a sash to absorb the blood from his side. Pain became his constant companion, but he kept it to himself, and it was noticeable to others only when he walked about. In obedience to his superiors, he had to undergo various intrusive medical examinations to ascertain the wounds' cause, but no medical rationale would ever explain them, nor the "celestial perfume" that surrounded him.

Despite all attempts to hide the stigmata, word spread, and throngs of faithful Roman Catholics soon flocked to San Giovanni Rotondo to attend Mass with the holy Pio and to wait in line to have him hear their confessions. Becoming known for his ability to "read" souls and discern intentions, he could also predict the future and effect cures and healings. He was also famous for the beauty of his Masses, which sometimes lasted for two hours. Between Mass and confessions, Pio's workday encompassed nineteen hours; his health at this point was fine, but he ate so sparingly for years—only 300 or 400 calories per day—that doctors believed a source of supernatural energy kept him alive.

Pio was also known to communicate with guardian angels and to bilocate. It is also believed that his warfare with demons became physical and that he was often bruised in his battles.

His gifts made him an "object" of intense devotion—indeed, at times, hysteria. When rumors arose that Pio was to be transferred to another monastery, the people of San Giovanni Rotondo barricaded the place—and threatened violence to anyone who took Pio away. People also tore at his robes when he passed by on the way to celebrate Mass, fought one another for the front seats in the chapel, and even sold cloths dipped in goat's blood to tourists hunting souvenirs of the stigmatized priest. Some of the diocesan priests, becoming jealous of Pio's popularity with their townspeople, conveyed false information to Rome, and as a result the Vatican took measures to downplay Pio's embarrassing notoriety. He was not allowed to correspond with his spiritual children after about 1922, and from 1931 to 1933 he was forbidden to say Mass in public or to hear confessions.

In imitation of Jesus, Pio had accepted a life of victimhood, offering his sacrifice for the salvation of souls everywhere. He had particular concern for those in purgatory. So he endured his "imprisonment" by communing with God and praying for his spiritual children and for others whose needs were made known to him, sometimes through supernatural means. After the ban was lifted on his public appearances—though not on his correspondence—he was able once again to exercise a wonderful ministry, effecting numerous conversions and serving as a "designer of souls." Though a few of his followers continued to display unchristian behavior around him, the majority of his visitors were sincere in their spiritual intentions.

Some say that it was due to Pio's supernatural intervention, but it is true that the destruction of World War II passed San Giovanni Rotondo by. Nevertheless, foreign GIs, particularly Americans, became aware of Padre Pio and brought stories of him home with them, with the result that his reputation, previously limited to a provincial area of Italy, spread throughout the world.

This proved beneficial for the town and monastery, for Padre Pio had envisioned building a first-class hospital for the care of the sick in San Giovanni Rotondo. This impoverished corner could not afford such a facility, but through his ministry Pio was able to collect donations from around the globe, and the hospital, called the Home for the Relief of Suffering, opened its doors in 1956.

Pio continued to minister to many people through the confessional, but by 1967 he was weakening. The stigmata also began to disappear, though the pain remained. By the time of his death on September 23, 1968, the wounds had completely vanished.

Yet the special ministry of this victim soul has not really ended, for the well-documented accounts of his amazing life continue to bring people to San Giovanni Rotondo, where they seek the truth and love that Blessed Padre Pio brought to all the souls he touched. And just as they inspired his spiritual children and confidants during his lifetime, his words— as the selections in this collection amply demonstrate—continue to be a source of profound inspiration for the faithful today.

—AFC

ℳY OWN LIFE

Did I not tell you
that Jesus wants me to suffer
without any consolation?
Has he not asked me
and chosen me to be one of his victims?
Our most sweet Jesus has really made me
understand the full significance of
being a victim.

LETTER TO PADRE AGOSTINO,
NOVEMBER 5, 1912

Oh, how sweet was the colloquy with paradise that morning! [...] The heart of Jesus and my own—allow me to use the expression—were fused. No longer were two hearts beating but only one. My own heart had disappeared, as a drop of water is lost in the ocean. Jesus was its paradise, its king. My joy was so intense and deep that I could bear no more and tears of happiness poured down my cheeks.

LETTER TO PADRE AGOSTINO, APRIL 18, 1912

Listen, now, to what happened to me last Friday. I was in the church making my thanksgiving after Mass, when I suddenly felt my heart wounded by a fiery dart, so sharp and ardent that I thought I should die.

[...] It seemed to me as if an invisible power were plunging my whole being into fire. Dear God! What fire! What delight!

I have experienced a great many of these transports of love, and for some time have remained, as it were, outside this world. On the other occasions, however, this fire was less intense, whereas this time another moment, another second, and my soul would have been separated from my body and would have gone to Jesus.

[...] Jesus has now withdrawn his fiery dart, but I am mortally wounded.

LETTER TO PADRE AGOSTINO, AUGUST 26, 1912

Whenever I ask him what have I done to deserve such consolations, he smiles and says repeatedly that nothing is refused to such an intercessor. In return he asks me for nothing but love, but do I not perhaps owe him this in gratitude?

Oh, my dear Father, if I could only make him happy just as he makes me happy! He is so much in love with my heart that he makes me burn with his divine fire, with the fire of his love. What is this fire that pervades my whole being? Dear Father, if Jesus makes us so happy on earth, what will heaven be like?

LETTER TO PADRE AGOSTINO, DECEMBER 3, 1912

The thought that at any moment I may lose Jesus distresses me in a way that I cannot explain; only a soul that loves Jesus sincerely can understand what this means.

LETTER TO PADRE AGOSTINO, DECEMBER 29, 1912

$\mathcal{I}$ addressed my usual prayer to him with greater confidence: "Oh, Jesus, if I could only love you, if I could only suffer as much as I should like in order to make you happy and make some kind of reparation for men's ingratitude towards you!"

But Jesus made his voice more clearly audible in my heart: "My son, love is recognized in suffering; you will feel it acutely in your soul and even more acutely in your body."

LETTER TO PADRE AGOSTINO, DECEMBER 29, 1912

$\mathcal{T}$he natural acts themselves, such as eating, drinking and sleeping, are a very great burden to me. My soul groans under this weight, for the hours pass too slowly for it. At the end of each day I feel as if relieved of a great weight and greatly comforted; but soon my soul falls back into deeper gloom at the thought of the many days of exile still to be endured. At these moments I am induced to cry out: Oh life, how cruel you are to me! How long you are! Oh life, no longer life to me but torment! Oh death, I do not know who can fear you, for through you life begins!

LETTER TO PADRE BENEDETTO, JULY 7, 1913

$\mathcal{M}$y dear Father, how hard it is to believe! May the Lord help me and not allow me to cast the shadow of doubt on what he has been pleased to reveal to us.

LETTER TO PADRE BENEDETTO, MARCH 8, 1916

$\mathcal{D}$ear Father, when will the sun shine in the heavens of my soul? Alas, I see myself astray in the deep dark night through which I am passing. But praise be to God, who never abandons anyone who hopes and places his trust in him!

LETTER TO PADRE AGOSTINO, AUGUST 15, 1916

$\mathcal{W}$hen will my heart find rest? I feel it is breaking and I don't know where to turn. If I could at least have the satisfaction of giving vent to this interior torment by tears, it would be some relief, but my sorrow is so great that it has turned my heart to stone.

I now understand, dear Jesus, why your Mother did not cry as she gazed at you on the Cross.

LETTER TO PADRE BENEDETTO, JANUARY 31, 1918

While I was hearing the boys' confessions on the evening of the 5th I was suddenly terrorized by the sight of a celestial person who presented himself to my mind's eye. He had in his hand a sort of weapon like a very long sharp-pointed steel blade which seemed to emit fire. At the very instant that I saw all this, I saw that person hurl the weapon into my soul with all his might. I cried out with difficulty and felt I was dying. I asked the boy to leave because I felt ill and no longer had the strength to continue.

This agony lasted uninterruptedly until the morning of the 7th. I cannot tell you how much I suffered during this period of anguish. Even my entrails were torn and ruptured by the weapon, and nothing was spared. From that day on I have been mortally wounded. I feel in the depths of my soul a wound that is always open and which causes me continual agony.

LETTER TO PADRE BENEDETTO, AUGUST 21, 1918

On the morning of the 20th of last month, in the choir, after I had celebrated Mass I yielded to a drowsiness similar to a sweet sleep. [...]

I saw before me a mysterious person similar to the one I had seen on the evening of

5 August. The only difference was that his hands and feet and side were dripping blood. This sight terrified me and what I felt at that moment is indescribable. I thought I should die and really should have died if the Lord had not intervened and strengthened my heart which was about to burst out of my chest.

The vision disappeared and I became aware that my hands, feet and side were dripping blood. Imagine the agony I experienced and continue to experience almost every day. The heart wound bleeds continually, especially from Thursday evening until Saturday. Dear Father, I am dying of pain because of the wounds and the resulting embarrassment I feel deep in my soul. I am afraid I shall bleed to death if the Lord does not hear my heartfelt supplication to relieve me of this condition. Will Jesus, who is so good, grant me this grace? Will he at least free me from the embarrassment caused by these outward signs? I will raise my voice and will not stop imploring him until in his mercy he takes away, not the wound or the pain, which is impossible since I wish to be inebriated with pain, but these outward signs which cause me such embarrassment and unbearable humiliation.

LETTER TO PADRE BENEDETTO, OCTOBER 22, 1918

THE SACRAMENTS

It is easier for the earth to exist without the sun than without the holy sacrifice of the Mass.

ARCHIVES OF PADRE PIO

*W*hen you are uncertain, or rather, in doubt as to whether or not you mortally offended God—may God preserve you from this—act as follows: Make an act of contrition and go forward. What else?

LETTER TO ELENA VENTRELLA, UNDATED

*N*ever undertake any work or any action without first raising your mind to God and directing to him with a pure intention the action you are about to perform. You should do likewise at the end of every action. Examine yourself as to whether you have done everything with the right intention you had at the beginning[,] and if you find you have been at fault, then ask pardon of the Lord with humility while making a firm resolution to correct your faulty conduct.

LETTER TO RAFFAELINA CERASE, DECEMBER 17, 1914

*C*ontinue to receive Communion, and don't worry about not being able to receive the sacrament of penance. Jesus will prize your goodwill. Remember what I have told you so often: as long as we are not certain of being in serious sin, we need not abstain from Communion.

FRAGMENTS OF LIGHT

*R*EMEMBRANCE OF MY FIRST MASS

Jesus
My breath—My life
Today, trembling, I elevate You
In a mystery of love
With You let me be for the world
The Way—The Truth—The Life
And for You a holy priest
A perfect victim.

LETTER TO ASSUNTA DI TOMASO,
OCTOBER 22, 1916

My dear daughter, I think that the holy Eucharist is a great means through which to aspire to perfection. But we must receive it with the desire and intention of removing from the heart all that is displeasing to him with whom we wish to dwell.

LETTER TO MARIA GARGANI, JULY 27, 1917

Every holy Mass, heard with devotion, produces in our souls marvelous effects, abundant spiritual and material graces which we, ourselves, do not know.

PADRE PIO ANSWERS...

In the most holy sacrament of the Eucharist, in this sacrament of love, we have true life, a blessed life, and true happiness. Because in it we receive, not only those graces that perfect us, but the very author of these graces.

LETTER TO GRAZIELLA PANNULLO, DECEMBER 30, 1921

$\mathcal{I}$ should like to shed, not a few tears, but torrents of tears when faced with the mystery of a God Victim. We priests are butchers of Jesus during the Mass, while all of paradise reverently descends on the altar.

I never tire of standing so long, and could not become tired, because I am not standing, but am on the cross with Christ, suffering with him.

The holy Mass is a sacred union of Jesus and myself. I suffer unworthily all that was suffered by Jesus who deigned to allow me to share in his great enterprise of human redemption.

ARCHIVES OF PADRE PIO

PRAYER AND MEDITATION

You ought to ask our Lord

for just one thing: to love him.

All the rest should be thanksgiving.

LETTER TO PADRE BENEDETTO,
NOVEMBER 20, 1921

$\mathcal{B}$y studying books, one seeks God; by praying, one finds him.

FOR HISTORY

$\mathcal{O}$ne does not achieve salvation without prayer; one does not win the battle without prayer. The choice is yours.

LETTERS OF PADRE PIO

$\mathcal{L}$et us pray fervently, humbly and perseveringly. The Lord is a father, the most tender and best of fathers. He cannot fail to be moved when his children appeal to him.

LETTER TO RAFFAELINA CERASE, JUNE 8, 1915

$\mathcal{P}$ut into practice the saying of David: *Lift up your hands to the holy place and bless the Lord!* Yes, my daughter, let us bless the Lord with all our hearts, and let us bless him always, and pray that he may be our guide, our ship and our port.

LETTER TO VITTORINA VENTRELLA, UNDATED

*J*esus has prayed to teach us also that when our soul finds itself in desolation like his, we should seek consolation from heaven only in prayer to sustain us in the sacrifice.

THE AGONY OF JESUS IN THE
GARDEN OF GETHSEMANE

*P*ray with your heart and with your mind. It is useless to pray only with the heart, without the mind. If we pray without paying attention to what we are saying, we will have the curse of the Lord, not his blessing. So when you pray, be very careful to pray with your heart and your mind, with *all* your soul.

WORDS TO PIETRUCCIO

*P*rayer is the best weapon we have; it is a key that opens God's heart. You must speak to Jesus, not only with your lips, but also with your heart; actually, on certain occasions, you should speak with only your heart.

ADVICE AND EXHORTATIONS OF
PADRE PIO OF PIETRELCINA

*F*requently repeat the divine words of our dear Master, "Thy will be done on earth as it is in heaven." May this beautiful exclamation always be in your heart and on your lips in all the vicissitudes of life. Repeat it in affliction. Repeat it in temptation and in the trials to which Jesus will be pleased to subject you. Repeat it still when you find yourself immersed in the ocean of Jesus' love. This will be your anchor and your salvation.

LETTER TO A SPIRITUAL DAUGHTER

*I*f you can speak to the Lord, speak to him, praise him; if you cannot speak because you are exhausted, don't worry. When approaching the Lord, lock yourself in your room, and like a courtier, revere him. He will see you and be pleased with your presence; he will accept your silence[;] then, on some other occasion, he will console you by taking your hand, speaking to you, and walking with you along the paths in his garden of prayers.

FRAGMENTS OF LIGHT

$\mathcal{R}$emember that one thing only is necessary, to be close to Jesus. Tell me, my dear daughters, you know well that at the birth of our Lord, the shepherds heard the divine and angelic singing of the heavenly spirits. Scripture tells us this, but it does not say that the Virgin, his Mother and Saint Joseph, who were closest to the Infant, heard the voices of the angels or saw those miraculous splendors. On the contrary, instead of hearing the angels singing, they heard the Child crying, and saw by the light of a poor lamp, the eyes of this divine Infant all wet with tears and trembling with cold.

Now, I ask you, wouldn't you have chosen to be in that dark stable filled with the cries of the little Child, rather than beside yourselves with joy, with the shepherds at this sweet heavenly melody, and the beauty of this admirable splendor? Yes, undoubtedly, you too would have exclaimed with Saint Peter: *"It is good that we are here."*

LETTER TO THE VENTRELLA SISTERS,
OCTOBER 1, 1917

$\mathcal{A}$ Christian soul never lets a day go by without meditating on the passion of Jesus Christ.

THE TIME-PIECE OF THE
PASSION OF OUR LORD JESUS CHRIST

$\mathcal{W}$hen there is no time for both, meditation is to be preferred to vocal prayer, because it is more fruitful.

COUNSELS

$\mathcal{H}$e who never meditates is like a person who never looks in the mirror; therefore, not knowing that he is untidy, he goes out looking disorderly. The person who meditates and directs his thoughts to God, who is the mirror of his soul, tries to know his faults, attempts to correct them, moderates his impulses, and puts his conscience in order.

FOR HISTORY

*H*elp yourself [...] by reading holy books. I earnestly desire to see you reading such books at all times, for this reading provides excellent food for the soul and conduces to great progress along the path of perfection, by no means inferior to what we obtain through prayer and holy meditation. In prayer and meditation it is we ourselves who speak to the Lord, while in holy reading it is God who speaks to us. Try to treasure these holy readings as much as you can and you will very soon be aware of a spiritual renewal within you.

LETTER TO RAFFAELINA CERASE, JULY 14, 1914

*W*hy do you distress yourself because you cannot meditate, as you suppose? Meditation is a means to rise to God, but not an end. The final purpose of meditation is the love of God and one's neighbor. Love the first with all your soul and without reservation; love the second as another self, and you will have arrived at the final purpose of meditation.

COUNSELS

When you do not succeed in meditating well do not for this reason cease to do your duty. If there are many distractions do not lose heart. Make a meditation of patience; you will profit all the same. Fix the time, the length of your meditation, and do not rise from your place until you have finished it, even at the cost of being crucified.

COUNSELS

Go with your mind to Calvary and think and meditate on the Victim who offers himself to divine Justice, absorbing the price of your redemption.

COUNSELS

*M*ake a preparation for the entire day, briefly in the morning, offering to God everything you do throughout the day: Then, mental prayer ordinarily before approaching holy Communion, for about one hour. [...] In the evening, before going to bed, examine your conscience and consecrate yourself to God, offering him the rest you are about to take. From after lunch onwards, choose another specific time in order to withdraw into yourself before God, with a further hour's meditation.

Do the spiritual reading whenever it suits you best, for not less than half an hour. [...]

During the day, as you go about your daily business, examine yourself as often as you can, to see whether your love has gone too far ahead; whether it is disorganized or if you always hold on to the Lord with one hand.

LETTER TO ERMINIA GARGANI, JANUARY 12, 1917

$\mathscr{I}$t would be wise to remember that the graces and joys of prayer are not earthly waters, but celestial waters; therefore, all of our endeavors are insufficient to cause a downpour. Of course, the utmost diligence is necessary, but so are humility and tranquillity. One must keep one's heart open towards heaven, waiting for the celestial dew.

ARCHIVES OF PADRE PIO

𝒯HE DARK NIGHT
OF THE SOUL

𝒯he spiritual combats instead of dying down
are pressing on me relentlessly.
Darkness is followed by darkness
and spiritual blindness has become
pitch darkness for me.

Dear God! What is to become of me? Will I
have to pass the threshold leading to eternity
without ever seeing a ray of light?
When is the sun to rise for me?

LETTER TO PADRE AGOSTINO, MARCH 25, 1916

You are suffering and are right to complain. By all means complain and in a loud voice, but fear nothing. The victim of Love is impatient to possess it; it must cry out that it can take no more and that it is impossible to resist the treatment of the Beloved who wants her and leaves her and leaves her while he wants her.

LETTER TO MARIA GARGANI, APRIL 28, 1919

You are trying to measure, understand, feel and touch this love which you have for God, but, my dear sister, you must accept as certain that the more a soul loves God the less it feels this love.

LETTER TO RAFFAELINA CERASE, MAY 19, 1914

You seek your God; you sigh for him, call him but cannot see any trace of him. God seems to hide himself; to abandon you! But, I repeat, do not fear. Jesus is with you then also, and you are in him and with him. […] In time of darkness, tribulation, anxiety of spirit, Jesus is with you. […]

Even our Lord on the cross complained of the Father's abandonment. But did the Father ever, and could he ever really have abandoned his Son? These are the supreme trials of the spirit. Jesus wants them, so Fiat! Pronounce this fiat with resignation whenever you are in that state of trial and do not fear.

LETTER TO ANTONIETTA VONA, JUNE 28, 1918

*D*on't be discouraged if you experience spiritual dryness. This does not mean that the Lord has abandoned you, as that ugly wretch, Satan, would unfortunately have you believe. You are too dear to the heart of Jesus and all that is happening in your soul is due to the exquisiteness of Jesus' love for you. He wants you entirely for himself, he wants you to place all your trust and all your affection in him alone, and it is precisely for this reason that he sends you this spiritual aridity, to unite you more closely to him, to rid you of certain little attachments which do not appear as such to us and which, in many cases, we do not even recognize or detect.

I am aware that the state of the soul placed in such straits is a sad one, when it really seems to us that all is ended and that the Lord has left us for good because he is tired of bearing with us. Instead, things are quite different. The Lord is never so pleased with us as he is at such times as this. He is always there, close to us, or rather within us, invisibly encouraging us to endure the combat. Don't worry, then, because the Lord will fight for you and will never withdraw from you.

LETTER TO RAFFAELINA CERASE, JULY 14, 1914

*H*ow is it possible that the fountain of living water which issues from the divine Heart should be far from a soul that rushes to it like a thirsty hart? It is true that this soul may also fail to believe it because it feels continually consumed by an unquenchable and insatiable thirst. But what of that? Does this, perhaps, go to show that the soul does not possess God? Quite the opposite.

This happens because the soul has not yet reached the end of its journey and is not yet totally immersed in the eternal fountain of his divine love, which will happen in the kingdom of glory. Let us therefore love to quench our thirst at this fountain of living water and go forward all the time along the way of divine love. But let us also be convinced, my daughter, that our souls will never be satisfied here below. In fact it would be disastrous for us if, at a certain stage of our journey, we were to feel satisfied, for it would be a sign that we thought we had reached our goal and in this we would be deceived.

LETTER TO RAFFAELINA CERASE,
OCTOBER 21, 1915

*D*on't be bewildered if the night becomes deeper and darker for you. Don't be frightened if you are unable to see, with the eyes of the body, the serene sky that surrounds your soul. But look above, elevating yourself above yourself, and you will see a light shining, that participates in the light of the eternal Sun.

LETTER TO ASSUNTA DI TOMASO,
OCTOBER 22, 1916

*M*y dearest daughter, I see that all the seasons of the year can be found in your soul. Sometimes you feel the winter of so much sterility, distraction, listlessness and boredom; sometimes the dews of the month of May with the perfume of holy little flowers; sometimes you experience the colors of the desire to please God. Nothing remains but the autumn which, as you see, does not bear too much fruit, but it often happens that, when the grain is threshed and the grapes crushed one finds the harvest is greater than it had promised!

My daughter, you would like it to be eternally spring and summer! But no, my daughter, these rotations are necessary both internally and externally. Only in heaven will everything be spring as regards beauty[,] autumn as regards enjoyment and summer as regards love. There will be no winter, but here winter is necessary in order to practice abnegation and those beautiful little virtues which are practiced in time of sterility.

Letter to Maria Gargani, May 18, 1918

*E*xile according to God's will is better than the tabernacles of Jacob without his will.

Letter to Padre Agostino, May 4, 1917

*T*he most beautiful *Credo* is the one we pronounce when we are in darkness, in the hour of sacrifice and sorrow, in the supreme effort of an inflexible will for what is good. This is the one that as a flash of lightning breaks the darkness of the soul; the one that in the midst of a raging storm lifts up the soul and leads it to God.

A CITY ON A MOUNTAIN

*L*ive completely at peace because there will be light.

LETTER TO ANNITA RODOTE, OCTOBER 31, 1915

THE CROSS

You suffer, but believe also that
Jesus himself suffers in you and for you.

COUNSELS

$\mathcal{T}$he prototype, the example on which one should reflect and model one's self is Jesus Christ. But Jesus chose the cross as his standard, so he wants all his followers to tread the path to Calvary, carrying the cross and then dying stretched out on it. Only this way do we reach salvation.

LETTER TO MARIA GARGANI, SEPTEMBER 4, 1916

$\mathcal{Y}$ou complain because the same trials are constantly returning. But look here, Father, what have you to fear? Are you afraid of the divine Craftsman who wants to perfect his masterpiece in this way? Would you like to come from the hands of such a magnificent Artist as a mere sketch and no more? Yet you yourself like to produce perfect words!

I laugh and laugh loudly at the manner in which God treats you. Listen, Father, just keep cheerful, be at peace and let God do as he pleases.

LETTER TO PADRE BENEDETTO, JANUARY 1, 1921

*E*ach soul must learn to allow itself to be handled, planed and smoothed by the divine Spirit, when he also acts as a doctor of our souls so that, having been well planed and smoothed, they can be united and joined to the will of God. [...]

Lovingly, sweetly and lovably make this resolution: either to die or be cured. And as you don't want to die spiritually, try to be healed perfectly. And in order to be healed, desire to bear the treatment and correction of the divine Doctor, and beseech him not to spare you in anything in order to save you.

<small>LETTER TO MARIA GARGANI, DECEMBER 10, 1917</small>

*I*n order to reach our final goal, we must follow our divine Leader, who usually leads chosen souls by the path he himself has trodden and by no other; by the path, I tell you, of self-denial and suffering: *If any man would come after me, let him deny himself and take up his cross and follow me.* Should you not deem yourself fortunate to see yourself treated in this way by Jesus? Foolish are those who fail to fathom the secret of the cross.

<small>LETTER TO RAFFAELINA CERASE, AUGUST 15, 1914</small>

$\mathcal{H}$appy are we who, contrary to our every merit, are already on the hill of Calvary by divine mercy. We have already been made worthy to follow the heavenly Master; we have already been numbered amongst that blessed group of chosen souls, and all this through a most special act of divine mercy on the part of the heavenly Father. Let us not allow this blessed group to disappear from sight, but let us always keep ourselves tightly united to them, fearing neither the weight of the cross we have to carry, the long journey to be made, nor the steep hill which we must climb.

LETTER TO THE VENTRELLA SISTERS, DECEMBER 3, 1916

$\mathcal{W}$e must never separate the Cross from Jesus' love; otherwise it would become a weight which in our weakness we could not carry.

LETTER TO PADRE AGOSTINO, JULY 1, 1915

$\mathcal{W}$e do not want to accept the fact that suffering is necessary for our souls, that the cross must be our daily bread. Just as the body is in need of nutrition, so is the soul in need of the cross which, day by day, purifies it, and detaches it from the mundane. We do not wish to understand that God neither wants, nor is able, to save and sanctify us without the cross; the more he calls a soul to him, the more he sanctifies it by means of the cross.

PADRE PIO ANSWERS...

$\mathcal{H}$ow unbearable is pain when suffered far from the Cross, but how sweet and bearable it becomes when it is offered close to the cross of Jesus!

LETTER TO PADRE AGOSTINO, MAY 20, 1915

$\mathcal{T}$he Lord loads us and sets us free from our load, for when he bestows a cross on one of his chosen ones, he strengthens that soul to such an extent that by bearing the weight of this cross he is relieved of it.

LETTER TO PADRE AGOSTINO, DECEMBER 15, 1917

If we realize that every victory we obtain has a corresponding degree of eternal glory, how can we fail to rejoice, dear Father, when we find ourselves obliged to face many trials in the course of our life?

LETTER TO PADRE AGOSTINO, MARCH 25, 1918

Jesus wants to toss and shake you, to thresh you like wheat in order that your spirit may be cleansed and purified as he wishes. Could grain be stored in the barn if it were not free from all husk and chaff? Could linen be stored in the owner's cupboard if it had not first been made quite spotless? So, too, must it be with the chosen soul.

LETTER TO RAFFAELINA CERASE, APRIL 11, 1914

To be on the cross with Jesus is infinitely more perfect than merely contemplating Jesus himself on the cross.

LETTER TO RAFFAELINA CERASE,
NOVEMBER 26, 1914

The cross will not be as heavy as the one carried by the only begotten Son of the heavenly Father. Jesus, who is infinitely merciful, will not fail to give you now and then a respite from the trial he has sent you. He is so good that he will never allow you to give in.

LETTER TO RAFFAELINA CERASE, JANUARY 23, 1915

This suffering is not a chastisement from God, but rather the fruit of the love with which he wants to render you similar to his Son. You are suffering, but believe also that Jesus is suffering in you, for you and with you. He is associating you in his passion and you, as a victim, must make up for your brothers and sisters that which is lacking in the passion of Jesus Christ. Let the thought that you are not alone in that agony, but rather in good company, be of comfort to you.

LETTER TO MARGHERITA TRESCA,
AUGUST 13, 1918

$\mathcal{I}$n moments of extreme distress you too pray to the heavenly Father that he might comfort and console you. If he is not pleased to do this, think of it no more, but arm yourself with new courage and undertake the work of your salvation on the cross, as if you were never to descend from it and were never to see your life becoming serene for you once again.

LETTER TO ANTONIETTA VONA, DECEMBER 6, 1917

$\mathcal{Y}$our tears were collected by the angels and were placed in a gold chalice, and you will find them when you present yourself before God.

"SEND ME YOUR GUARDIAN ANGEL"

$\mathcal{Y}$ou should be encouraged and comforted by the knowledge that we are not alone in our sufferings, for all the followers of the Nazarene scattered throughout the world suffer in the same manner and are all exposed like ourselves to the trials and tribulations of life.

LETTER TO RAFFAELINA CERASE,
NOVEMBER 26, 1914

The cross will never oppress you; its weight might cause you to stagger, but its strength will sustain you.

ARCHIVES OF PADRE PIO

Jesus is never without the cross, but the cross is never without Jesus.

ARCHIVES OF PADRE PIO

The God of Christians is the God of metamorphosis: you throw your pain in his lap, and retrieve peace; you throw your despair, and retrieve hope.

SAN GIOVANNI ROTONDO:
IN THE LIGHT OF FRANCISCANISM

Many suffer, but few know how to suffer well. Suffering is a gift from God; blessed is he who knows how to profit by it.

ARCHIVES OF PADRE PIO

$\mathcal{T}$he soul that is destined to reign with Jesus Christ in eternal glory [...] must be remodeled by the blows of hammer and chisel. But what are these blows of hammer and chisel by which the divine Artist prepares the stone, that is to say, the chosen soul? Dear sister, these strokes of the chisel are the shadows, fears, temptations, spiritual torments and agitation, with a dash of desolation and even of physical pain.

Thank the infinite mercy of the eternal Father, then, for treating your soul in this way, for it is destined to be saved.

LETTER TO RAFFAELINA CERASE, MAY 19, 1914

$\mathcal{T}$ribulations and trials have always been the heritage and the portion of chosen souls. The more Jesus intends to raise a soul up to perfection, the more he tries it by suffering. Rejoice, I say to you, in seeing yourself so privileged, in spite of your own unworthiness. The more you are afflicted, the more you ought to rejoice, because in the fire of tribulation the soul will become pure gold, worthy to be placed and to shine in the heavenly palace.

LETTER TO RAFFAELINA CERASE, JULY 14, 1914

GOD'S WILL

Let us adhere to the will of God.
Let this be the star on which
we rest our gaze throughout this
navigation, because in
that way we cannot but reach
the right port.

LETTER TO AN UNIDENTIFIED PERSON,
NOVEMBER 5, 1917

*F*iat! We must abandon life and everything we are, leaving it at the disposition of divine Providence, given that we do not live and do not belong to ourselves but to he who, in order to render us his, desired to make us entirely his in such a loving manner.

LETTER TO MARIA GARGANI, FEBRUARY 12, 1917

*L*et us pray and beseech God to let us understand his will. Let us see to it that our will desires nothing at all except his.

LETTER TO MARIA GARGANI, MAY 18, 1918

*D*o not believe that you would serve him better in a different state, because one only serves him well when one serves him as he wishes.

LETTER TO MARIA GARGANI, NOVEMBER 11, 1916

$\mathcal{T}$he ardent desire to be in eternal peace is good and holy. But it is necessary to moderate it by a complete resignation to the divine will. It is better to do the divine will on earth than to enjoy heaven.

Counsels

$\mathcal{M}$ake a particular effort to practice sweetness and submission to the will of God, not only where extraordinary matters are concerned, but also in the little daily events that occur. Make these acts not only in the morning, but also during the day and in the evening with a joyful and tranquil spirit. And if you should happen to fail in some way, humble yourself, make a new proposition, pick yourself up and carry on.

Letter to an unidentified person,
January 27, 1918

$\mathcal{D}$o not allow yourself to be overcome by discouragement if you don't always visibly see your every effort crowned. Jesus sees, rewards and commands good will and not good success, because the latter does not depend on human efforts and work.

LETTER TO ERMINIA GARGANI, FEBRUARY 16, 1921

$\mathcal{Y}$ou are distressed, moreover, that your will has no part in your resignation to the divine plan. Are you really sure of this statement? [...] Unfortunately, when you utter your act of acceptance of God's will you want to feel this in your heart also with a kind of perceptible sweetness. But have I not told you that the state of purgation in which the Lord has placed you consists precisely in stripping your soul of that delightful feeling it experiences in the service of God?

Consider Jesus' act of acceptance in the garden and how much it cost him, making him sweat a sweat of blood! Make this act yourself when things are going well and also when they go against you. Don't be upset and don't worry about the way in which you make your act. We know that nature shrinks from the cross when things are hard, but we cannot say the soul is not submissive to God's will when we see it carrying out that will in spite of the strong pull it feels in the opposite direction. [...]

If your will flees from rebellion you may be certain that it has tacitly or expressly submitted to God's will and consequently that the will, in its own way, has uttered its act of acceptance.

LETTER TO RAFFAELINA CERASE,
JANUARY 30, 1915

*D*o not undertake any course of action, not even the most lowly and insignificant, without first offering it to God.

ARCHIVES OF PADRE PIO

*G*od is served only when he is served according to his will.

ARCHIVES OF PADRE PIO

*L*et us always be prepared to recognize in every event of life the most wise order of divine Providence. Let us adore it and be ready to conform our will in all things and at all times to the will of God. In this way we shall give glory to the heavenly Father and everything will be to our advantage for eternal life.

LETTER TO RAFFAELINA CERASE,
FEBRUARY 23, 1915

*G*od, who has bestowed so many benefits on us, is satisfied with such a very insignificant gift as that of our will. Let us offer it to him along with the divine Master himself in that most sublime prayer, the *Our Father: Thy will be done on earth as it is in heaven.* Let us offer this will of ours with the same sentiment with which our divine Master offered it for us to his Father. Let us hand it over to him in a total offering and let us do this also in our daily life. Don't let us make our offering like those children who, when they have given away something precious as a gift, immediately or very soon regret what they have done and begin to cry and ask to have it back. Made in this way, our offering would be a mockery.

LETTER TO RAFFAELINA CERASE,
FEBRUARY 23, 1915

What else can we desire than God's will? What other wish can a soul have when it is consecrated to him? What else do you desire, then, if not that God's plan may be fulfilled in you? Take courage, therefore, and go forward on the path of divine love, with the firm conviction that the more fully your own will becomes united and conformed to God's will, the more you will advance towards perfection.

LETTER TO RAFFAELINA CERASE, JUNE 24, 1915

You, too, must learn to more greatly recognize and adore divine will in all the events of life. Often repeat the divine words of our dearest master: *Fiat voluntas Dei sicut in coelo et in terra.* Yes, let this beautiful exclamation always be in your heart and on your lips throughout all the events of your life. Say it in times of affliction; say it in times of temptation and during the trials to which Jesus wants to subject you. Say it again when you feel yourself submerged in the ocean of love for Jesus; it will be your anchor and salvation.

LETTER TO ANNITA RODOTE, FEBRUARY 6, 1915

$\mathcal{Y}$ou must not criticize the work of the Lord, but rather, you must humbly submit yourself to this divine work. Give total freedom to the workings of grace in you and remember never to be upset for any adverse event that could happen to you, knowing that this would be an impediment to the divine Spirit.

LETTER TO MARIA GARGANI, AUGUST 26, 1916

$\mathcal{I}$f possible[,] don't love the will of God merely when it conforms with yours, but rather love your will when and because it conforms to that of God.

LETTER TO MARIA GARGANI, FEBRUARY 19, 1918

$\mathcal{Y}$ou must [...] allow your divine Spouse to act in you and to lead you by the paths he chooses.

LETTER TO RAFFAELINA CERASE, JULY 14, 1914

$\mathcal{W}$here there is no obedience, there is no virtue; where there is no virtue, there is no good; where there is no good, there is no love; where there is no love, there is no God; and where there is no God, there is no paradise.

SPIRITUAL EXHORTATION

THE CHRISTIAN LIFE

Remember this:
the sinner who is ashamed to do evil
is closer to God than the upright man
who is ashamed to do good.

COUNSELS

*L*ive in such a way that you may be able to repeat at every moment with the apostle Saint Paul: *Be imitators of me, as I am of Jesus Christ.* Live in such a way, I repeat, that the world will be forced to say of you: "Here is Christ." Oh, for pity's sake, do not consider this an exaggeration! Every Christian who is a true imitator and follower of the fair Nazarene can and must call himself a second Christ and show forth most clearly in his life the entire image of Christ. Oh, if only all Christians were to live up to their vocation, this very land of exile would be changed into a paradise!

LETTER TO RAFFAELINA CERASE, MARCH 30, 1915

*G*od commands us to love him not as much and as he deserves, because he knows our limitations and therefore doesn't ask us to do what we cannot, but rather, he commands us to love him in accordance with our strength, with all our soul, all our mind and all our heart.

LETTER TO AN UNIDENTIFIED PERSON, JUNE 3, 1917

$\mathcal{H}$oliness means getting above ourselves; it means perfect mastery of all our passions. It means having real and continual contempt for ourselves and for the things of the world to the point of preferring poverty rather than wealth, humiliation rather than glory, suffering rather than pleasure. Holiness means loving our neighbor as ourself for love of God. In this connection holiness means loving those who curse us, who hate and persecute us, and even doing good to them. Holiness means living humbly, being disinterested, prudent, just, patient, kind, chaste, meek, diligent, carrying out one's duties for no other reason than that of pleasing God and receiving from him alone the reward we deserve.

Briefly, Raffaelina, holiness contains in itself the power to transform a man into God, according to the language of the holy books.

LETTER TO RAFFAELINA CERASE,
DECEMBER 30, 1915

$\mathcal{W}$e must beware of giving priority to what is advantageous to ourselves rather than what benefits others, because this preference for what is profitable to us rather than to others always tends necessarily to the violation of the beautiful bond of love, a bond which must always unite Christian souls, for love, as Saint Paul says, *binds everything together in perfect harmony*.

LETTER TO RAFFAELINA CERASE,
NOVEMBER 4, 1914

$\mathcal{N}$ever complain about offenses no matter where they come from; remember that Jesus was overwhelmed by the infamy and malice of the people whom he, himself, had helped.

Forgive everyone, with Christian charity, bearing in mind the example of our divine Master who asked his heavenly Father to forgive even those who crucified him.

ARCHIVES OF PADRE PIO

*O*ne can promote God's glory and work for the salvation of souls by means of a truly Christian life, by praying without ceasing that "his kingdom come," that his name "be hallowed," that "we may not be led into temptation" and that he "deliver us from evil."

This is what you ought to do, offering yourself continually to the Lord for this purpose. [...]

You may be perfectly sure that this is the highest form of apostolate that anyone can carry on in the Church of God.

LETTER TO RAFFAELINA CERASE,
NOVEMBER 4, 1914

A man who, transcending himself, bends over the wounds of his misfortunate brother, raises to the Lord the most beautiful, the most noble prayer, made of sacrifice and love lived.

THOUGHTS FOR THE RELIEF OF SUFFERING

*O*ne single act of love on the part of man, one single act of charity, is so great in God's eyes that he could not repay it even with the immense gift of the entire creation! Love is the spark of God in man's soul, it is the very essence of God personified in the Holy Spirit. To God we owe *all* our love, which, to be adequate, ought to be infinite. But this cannot be, because God alone is infinite. We must at least give our whole being to love, to charity. Our actions must be such that our Lord may say to us, "I was hungry and you gave me to eat; I was suffering and you cared for me and comforted me."

To carry out this ideal of our Lord, we must be quite forgetful of self. Rising above selfishness, we must bow down to the sufferings and the wounds of our fellowmen. We must make them our own, knowing how to suffer with our brethren for the love of God. We must know how to instill hope into their hearts and bring back a smile to their lips, having restored a ray of light into their souls. Then we shall be offering God the most beautiful, the most noble of prayers, because our prayer will have sprung from sacrifice. It will be the very essence of love, the unselfish gift of all that we are in body and soul.

WORDS TO DOCTORS KISVARDAY,
SANGUINETTI, AND DE VICO,
JANUARY, 1940

*J*esus calls the poor and simple shepherds by means of angels to manifest himself to them. He calls the learned men by means of their science. And all of them, moved interiorly by grace, hasten to adore him.

He calls all of us with divine inspirations and he communicates himself to us with his grace. How many times has he not lovingly invited us also? And with what promptitude have we replied?

My God, I blush and am filled with confusion at having to reply to such a question.

LETTER TO A SPIRITUAL CHILD

*W*e must make an effort to acquire this beautiful virtue of simplicity and to hold it in great esteem. Jesus said: *Unless you turn and become like children, you will never enter the kingdom of heaven.* But before he taught us this by his words he had already put it into practice. He became a child and gave us the example of that simplicity he was to teach us later also by his words.

LETTER TO PADRE AGOSTINO, JULY 10, 1915

$\mathcal{I}$ myself cannot see how a person can become proud on account of the gifts he recognizes in himself. It seems to me that the richer he sees himself to be, the more reason he has to humble himself before the Lord, for the Lord's gifts increase and he can never fully repay the giver of all good things.

LETTER TO RAFFAELINA CERASE, JANUARY 30, 1915

$\mathcal{O}$h, whenever the tempter wants you to be puffed up with pride, say to yourself: all that is good in me I have received from God on loan and I should be a fool to boast of what is not mine.

LETTER TO RAFFAELINA CERASE, JANUARY 30, 1915

$\mathcal{H}$ave you ever seen a field of fully ripened grain? You can observe that certain ears appear to be tall and fertile; others, however, are bent to the ground. Try to pick the tall, the most vain; you will see that they are empty; if, however, you pick the lowest, the most humble, you will find them loaded with grain. From this you may deduce that vanity is empty.

ADVICE AND EXHORTATIONS OF
PADRE PIO OF PIETRELCINA

$\mathcal{W}$e must behave in those times of struggle as a violinist usually behaves. Whenever the poor person notices a discordance, he neither breaks the string nor gives up playing the violin, but he immediately lends his ear in order to discover from where the discordance comes. Then he patiently tightens or loosens the string accordingly.

Well then, you too behave in this way. Don't become impatient at such wearisome matters, nor should you desire to break the string whenever you notice some discordance. But patiently humble yourself before God. Gently tighten or loosen the string of your heart before the heavenly Musician, in order that he might reorganize the concert.

LETTER TO MARIA GARGANI, NOVEMBER 22, 1916

$\mathcal{D}$on't allow any sadness to dwell in your soul, for sadness prevents the Holy Spirit from acting freely.

LETTER TO RAFFAELINA CERASE,
NOVEMBER 26, 1914

$\mathcal{S}$adness…is the slow death of the soul, and serves no purpose.

THE TIME-PIECE OF THE
PASSION OF OUR LORD JESUS CHRIST

$\mathcal{L}$et us not put off until tomorrow what we can do today. The graves are full of good intentions that never came to pass…besides, what assurance do we have that we will be alive tomorrow? Let us listen to the voice of our conscience, to the voice of the royal prophet: "Today, if you hear the voice of the Lord, do not turn a deaf ear." Let us come forth and treasure the fleeting moment which alone is ours. Let us not waste time, from one moment to another, because the latter is not yet ours.

TIME OF BIRTH

$\mathcal{L}$et us say to ourselves, with the full conviction of telling the truth, "My soul: begin today to do the good works which to date you have not done." Let us be moved by the presence of God.

TIME OF BIRTH

TEMPTATION AND SIN

As long as there remains a drop of blood
in our body, there will be a struggle
between right and wrong.

ARCHIVES OF PADRE PIO

$\mathcal{I}$ understand that temptations seem to stain rather than purify the soul, but this is not really the case. […I]t suffices to know what the great Saint Francis de Sales says, namely, that temptations are like the soap which when spread on the laundry seems to soil but in reality cleanses it.

LETTER TO RAFFAELINA CERASE, APRIL 11, 1914

$\mathcal{J}$esus permits the spiritual combat as a purification, not as a punishment. The trial is not unto death, but unto salvation.

LETTER TO PADRE AGOSTINO, MARCH 23, 1917

$\mathcal{A}$ soul who felt its weakness and had recourse to God for help, has never fallen. On the contrary, the soul is only defeated and overcome when, trusting in what it believes to be its abundant strength, it thinks it can always sustain and bear temptations. Thus it happens that the poor thing, out of presumption, believing it was touching the heavens, suddenly finds itself falling right to the doors of hell.

LETTER TO ANNITA RODOTE, APRIL 27, 1915

$\mathcal{D}$on't let temptations frighten you; they are the trials of the souls whom God wants to test when he sees they have the necessary strength to sustain the struggle, thus weaving the crown of glory with their own hands.

LETTER TO ANTONIETTA VONA,
SEPTEMBER 13, 1920

$\mathcal{N}$o chosen soul is free from temptations. Not even the apostle of the people who, after being taken away to paradise while still a traveling soul, was subjected to such a trial that Satan went so far as to hit him. Dear God! Who can read those pages without feeling one's blood freezing in one's veins?! How many tears, how many sighs, how many groans, how many prayers did this holy apostle raise, so that the Lord might withdraw this most painful trial from him! But what was Jesus' reply? Only this: "My grace is sufficient for you…"; "virtue in weakness," "one becomes perfect in weakness."

LETTER TO MARIA GARGANI, SEPTEMBER 4, 1916

The best means of guarding yourself against temptation are the following: —watch your senses to save them from dangerous temptation, avoid vanity, do not let your heart become exalted, convince yourself of the evil of complacency, flee away from hate, pray whenever possible.

COUNSELS

Remember that the devil has only one door by which to enter the soul: the will. There are no secret or hidden doors.

COUNSELS

If the devil makes a great deal of noise about you, rejoice, for this is a good sign. What we must dread is his peace and harmony with the human soul.

A CITY ON A MOUNTAIN

$\mathcal{D}$o not strain to overcome your temptations, because by straining, you might strengthen them; despise them, and do not dwell on them. Imagine that the crucified Jesus Christ is lying in your arms, on your breast, and while kissing his side, over and over again, say: "Here is my hope; here is the living source of my happiness! I shall hold you close, Oh my Jesus, and shall not let you go until you have made me secure."

FRAGMENTS OF LIGHT

$\mathcal{Y}$ou must by no means fear that the Lord will leave you at Satan's mercy. He is faithful and he never allows you to be tempted beyond your strength. He gives our enemy just as much power to torment you as serves his own fatherly plan for the sanctification of your soul and redounds to the greater glory of his divine Majesty. Hence you must be strong and cheerful in spirit, for the Lord is in the depths of your heart: he will fight along with you and for you. Who, then, will win the battle? Who is stronger than he is? Who will hold out against the King of the heavens? What is the creature, what is hell itself in front of the Lord?

Hold resolutely to the comforting thought that God is with you all the time and will never abandon you to Satan's attacks.

LETTER TO RAFFAELINA CERASE, APRIL 11, 1914

A person who does not love God does not pay any attention to God, does not feel afraid of not loving him and never troubles to think of God with the sincere desire to love him. Moreover, if the thought or idea of God sometimes comes into this person's mind, you will find that person dismissing the idea at once or almost at once.

Console yourself, I repeat, that as long as you are afraid that you do not love God and as long as you fear to offend him, you already love him and no longer offend him.

LETTER TO RAFFAELINA CERASE, MARCH 4, 1915

$\mathcal{D}$on't let these little imperfections discourage you. Try to be always watchful in order to avoid sin, but when you see that you fail in some way, don't become lost in useless complaining, but bend your knees before God; be embarrassed at your scarce fidelity; humble yourself greatly; ask our Lord's pardon; propose to be more watchful in the future, and then get up immediately and carry on […].

Convince yourselves, my most beloved daughters, that failings and little flights of the passions are inevitable as long as we are in this life, because, on this point, the great apostle Saint Paul cries out to heaven: "So I find it to be a law that when I want to do right, evil lies close at hand. For I delight in the law of God, in my inmost self, but I see in my members another law at war with the law of my mind, making me captive to the law of sin which dwells in my members. Wretched man that I am! Who will deliver me from this body of death?"

My daughters, we must resign ourselves to what we have inherited from our ancestors Adam and Eve. Self-love never dies before we do, but it will accompany us to the tomb. Dear God, my daughters, what unhappiness this is for us poor children of Eve! We must always feel the sensitive assaults of the passions, as long as we are in this miserable exile. But what of it? Should we perhaps become discouraged and renounce the life of heaven? No, most beloved daughters, let us take heart. It is sufficient for us not to consent with our deliberate will […].

LETTER TO RACHELINA RUSSO AND RACHELINA GISOLFI, SEPTEMBER 25, 1917

*D*on't be discouraged when you fall but animate yourself with new confidence and a more profound humility. Your becoming discouraged and disheartened after the fall is the work of the enemy; it means you surrender to him, and accept that you are beaten. You will not do this, therefore, because the grace of God is always vigilant in coming to your aid.

LETTER TO ANTONIETTA VONA, NOVEMBER 15, 1917

*N*othing is a sin unless it is committed voluntarily. Where there is no will, there is no sin, only human weakness.

FOR HISTORY

Sin, when followed by the profound pain of having committed it, by the loyal resolution of never repeating it, by the sharp realization that its great evil prompted the mercy of God, when after the hardest fibers of our hearts have been cut, results in an outburst of tears full of remorse and love. The sin itself, my son, becomes a step which brings us closer, which raises us, which more securely leads us to him.

THE GOOD SHEPHERD

Remember: The sinner who is sorry for his sins is closer to God than the just man who boasts of his good works.

ADVICE AND EXHORTATIONS OF
PADRE PIO OF PIETRELCINA

GOD'S MERCY

No one in this world merits anything;

it is the benevolent Lord,

in his infinite goodness

towards us, who grants everything,

because he pardons everything.

ADVICE AND EXHORTATIONS
OF PADRE PIO OF PIETRELCINA

No traveling soul can worthily love its God, but when this soul does everything it possibly can, and trusts in divine mercy, why should Jesus reject it? Didn't he command us to love God in accordance with our strength? When you have given and consecrated everything to God, why do you fear?

LETTER TO ERMINIA GARGANI, DECEMBER 14, 1916

The soul must be saddened by one thing alone, offending God, and even in this we must be very cautious. We must be sorry, it is true, for our failings, but with a calm sorrow while we continue to trust in the divine mercy.

LETTER TO PADRE AGOSTINO, JULY 10, 1915

Let us always bear in mind that if the Lord were to judge us according to strict justice, none of us, perhaps, would be saved. So let us make righteousness and peace exchange a kiss, which we shall obtain if we always tend towards mercy rather than justice, in imitation of our heavenly Father.

LETTER TO RAFFAELINA CERASE, APRIL 20, 1915

*I*f you were to judge men, and if God were to judge men as you usually judge yourself, everyone would perish and the very angels would have to be put out of paradise!

LETTER TO ERMINIA GARGANI, JANUARY 17, 1920

*E*ven sins themselves, which God keeps far from us by his goodness, are used for the good of those who serve him, by his divine Providence. If the holy King David had never sinned, he would never have acquired such a profound humility; nor would Mary Magdalene have so ardently loved Jesus if he had not forgiven her so many sins and if she had not committed them.

Consider, my dearest daughter, the work of this great mercy: It converts our sins into good, and with the venom of our sins makes a theriac which is healthy for our souls.

LETTER TO ANTONIETTA VONA, NOVEMBER 15, 1917

$\mathcal{G}$od can reject everything in a creature conceived in sin, which carries the indelible mark inherited from Adam, but he absolutely cannot reject the sincere desire to love him.

Therefore, if you cannot be sure of his heavenly mercy for other reasons, and you don't want to believe my assurances in the most sweet Lord, you must at least convince yourself for this reason: that is, that you sincerely desire to love God.

LETTER TO THE VENTRELLA SISTERS,
DECEMBER 7, 1916

$\mathcal{Y}$ou are loved by Jesus and Jesus has already forgiven your sins, so there can be no further reason for your spirit to be depressed. Your desire to convince yourself to the contrary is truly a waste of time; it is an offense to the heart of this most tender Lover of ours.

LETTER TO MARIA GARGANI, AUGUST 26, 1916

$\mathcal{G}$od does not reject sinners, but rather, grants them his grace, erecting the throne of his glory on their abjection and vileness.

LETTER TO ERMINIA GARGANI, AUGUST 28, 1918

$\mathcal{B}$efore the Lord abandons us, we should have to abandon him; in a word, we should first have to close the door of our heart to him, and even then, how many times does he not stretch out his hand to us to arrest our headlong dash towards the precipice! How many times, when we had abandoned him, has he not readmitted us to his loving embrace!

LETTER TO RAFFAELINA CERASE, JULY 28, 1914

$\mathcal{D}$ivine Goodness not only does not reject penitent souls, but even goes in search of obstinate souls.

ADVICE AND EXHORTATIONS OF
PADRE PIO OF PIETRELCINA

*I*n our thoughts, and in confession, we must not dwell on sins that were previously confessed. Because of our contrition, Jesus forgave them at the tribunal of penitence. It was there that he faced us and our destitution, like a creditor standing before an insolvent debtor. With a gesture of infinite generosity, he tore up and destroyed the promissory notes which we signed with our sins, and which we would certainly not have been able to pay without the help of his divine clemency. To dwell on those sins, wanting to unearth them again only because we wish to be pardoned again, only because we doubt that they have really been generously remitted, would result, perhaps, in a lack of trust in the goodness which he proved by his tearing up the documents of debt, which we contracted by our sins.... Dwell on them, if it is a source of comfort to your soul, but also dwell on your offenses against justice, wisdom, against the infinite mercy of God; dwell on them only to shed on them the redemptive tears of remorse and love.

BETWEEN THE MYSTERIES OF SCIENCE
AND THE LIGHT OF FAITH

*H*ave you not for sometime loved the Lord? Do you not love him now? Do you not long to love him forever? Therefore: Do not fear! Even conceded that you had committed all the sins of this world, Jesus repeats to you: Many sins are forgiven thee because thou hast loved much!

COUNSELS

*H*e wants our miseries to be the throne of his mercy, and your impotence, the seat of his omnipotence. Where did God place the divine strength he had given to Samson but in his hair, his weakest point?

LETTER TO THE VENTRELLA SISTERS,
OCTOBER 1, 1917

*M*ay whatever God has ordained for me come to pass, but in any event I will always hope in him and raise ever louder to him my cry: *Even if you were to slay me, I would hope in you.*

LETTER TO PADRE AGOSTINO, AUGUST 25, 1915

*C*ontinue calmly and rest upon the divine Heart without the slightest fear, because there you are well sheltered from the storms and not even God's justice can reach you.

LETTER TO PADRE AGOSTINO, SEPTEMBER 27, 1916

I understand very well that nobody can worthily love God, but when a person does all he can himself and trusts in the divine mercy, why should Jesus reject one who is seeking him like this? Has he not commanded us to love God with all the strength we have? Well, then, if you have given and consecrated everything you have to God, why are you afraid? Isn't it a real waste of time to dwell on it, a plot prepared by the enemy of our salvation?

LETTER TO RAFFAELINA CERASE, APRIL 20, 1915

*C*onfide and abandon yourself totally in the arms of divine mercy.

LETTER TO ELENA BANDINI, AUGUST 14, 1921

GOD'S PROVIDENCE

My past, Oh Lord, to your Mercy;

my present, to your Love;

my future, to your Providence!

COUNSELS

$\mathcal{R}$ely on Jesus for everything and all will work out well.

LETTER TO FRIEDA FOLGER, AUGUST 28, 1920

$\mathcal{H}$ave no fear at all about any future harm which could happen to you in this world, because perhaps it might not happen to you at all, but in any event if it were to come upon you, God would give you the strength to bear it.

LETTER TO ANTONIETTA VONA,
NOVEMBER 15, 1917

$\mathcal{S}$tay in the boat in which our Lord has placed you and let the storm come. You will not perish. It appears to you that Jesus is sleeping, but let it be so. Don't you know that if he sleeps, his heart vigilantly watches over you? Let him sleep, but at the right time he will awaken to restore your calm. Scripture tells us that dearest Saint Peter was frightened, and trembling, he exclaimed: "Oh Lord, save me!" And our Lord, taking him by the hand, replied: "Oh man of little faith, why did you doubt?" My daughter, observe this holy apostle. He walks with dry feet on the water; the waves and winds do not submerge him, but the fear of the winds and waves discourages and disheartens him. Fear is an evil worse than the evil itself.

Oh daughter of little faith, what do you fear? Isn't he watching over you? You are walking on the sea and you find the wind and waves, but isn't it enough to be with Jesus? What is there to fear? But if fear takes you by surprise, cry out aloud: "Oh Lord, save me!" He will stretch out his hand to you; hold on to it tightly and joyfully walk on the stormy sea of life.

LETTER TO AN UNIDENTIFIED PERSON,
DECEMBER 27, 1917

*L*et the world turn topsy-turvy, everything be in darkness and Mount Sinai all aflame, covered with lightning, thunder: God is with you. But if God lives in the darkness and Mount Sinai all aflame, covered with lightning, thunder, and noise, will we not be safe near him?

COUNSELS

$\mathscr{A}$bandon yourself totally in the arms of the divine goodness of the heavenly Father and do not fear, because your fear would be more ridiculous than that of a child in his mother's womb.

$\mathscr{B}$e tranquil because Jesus is with you and will never fail to assist you.

$\mathscr{S}$et aside all anxiety, for it is the most treacherous betrayer where true virtue and devotion are concerned. It seems to inspire us for good works, but it is not so, because it soon causes us to grow discouraged. For a while it does make us run, but only to see us stumble. For this reason we must shun anxiety on every occasion […].

$\mathcal{T}$o doubt is the greatest insult to the Divinity.

COUNSELS

$\mathcal{T}$o be worried because something we have done has not turned out in accordance with our pure intention shows a lack of humility. This is a clear sign that the person concerned has not entrusted the success of his action to the divine assistance but has depended too much on his own strength.

LETTER TO RAFFAELINA CERASE,
DECEMBER 17, 1914

$\mathcal{H}$umble yourself [...] at the delightful thought that you are in the divine arms of Jesus, the best of fathers, like a little infant in its mother's arms, and sleep peacefully with the certainty that you are being guided towards the destination which will be to your greatest advantage. How can we be afraid to remain in such loving arms when our entire being is consecrated to God?

LETTER TO RAFFAELINA CERASE, MARCH 29, 1914

$\mathcal{L}$ive calmly and do not worry excessively, because in order to work more freely in us, the Holy Spirit needs tranquillity and calm. And for you, every anxious thought is a mistake, as you have no reason to fear. It is the Lord who works within you and you must do nothing except leave the door of your heart wide open so that he might work as he pleases.

LETTER TO MARIA GARGANI, SEPTEMBER 16, 1916

$\mathcal{Y}$ou say well that you see nothing and find yourself in a burning thorn bush. The thorn bush burns, the entire air is filled with smoke and the spirit sees nothing. But God nevertheless speaks and is present to the soul that listens, understands, loves, trembles.

COUNSELS

$\mathcal{N}$ever fall back on yourself alone, but place all your trust in God and don't be too eager to be set free from your present state. Let the Holy Spirit act within you. Give yourself up to all his transports and have no fear. He is so wise and gentle and discreet that he never brings about anything but good. How good this Holy Spirit, this Comforter, is to all, but how supremely good he is to those who seek him!

LETTER TO RAFFAELINA CERASE, MARCH 29, 1914

$\mathcal{D}$o not anticipate the problems of this life with apprehension, but, rather, with a perfect hope that God, to whom you belong, will free us from them accordingly. He has defended you up to now. Simply hold on tightly to the hand of his divine providence and he will help you in all events, and when you are unable to walk, he will lead you, don't worry.

LETTER TO ERMINIA GARGANI, APRIL 23, 1918

I am oppressed by the uncertainty of my future, but I cherish the lively hope of seeing my dreams fulfilled, because the Lord cannot place thoughts and desires in a person's soul if he does not really intend to fulfill them, to gratify these longings which he alone has caused.

LETTER TO PADRE AGOSTINO, OCTOBER 4, 1915

A lways look ahead without troubling too much in reflecting on the dangers you see at a distance. These seem to you to be an enormous army, but they are nothing: they are only pruned willow trees. […] Don't worry about tomorrow, think only of doing good today, and when tomorrow comes, it will be today and then it is time enough to think of it.

LETTER TO ERMINIA GARGANI, MARCH 3, 1917

D on't think about tomorrow's events, because the same heavenly Father who takes care of you today, will do the same tomorrow and forever.

LETTER TO ERMINIA GARGANI, APRIL 23, 1918

$\mathcal{I}$n the hour of trial don't tire yourself, my daughter, in trying to find God. He is within you even then, in a most intimate manner. He is with you in your groanings and searching, just like a mother who urges her little child to seek her while she is behind him and it is precisely her hands that encourage him to reach her, in vain.

LETTER TO MARIA GARGANI, AUGUST 12, 1918

$\mathcal{I}$f there is nothing in a soul but a longing to love its God, everything is there already, God himself is there, because God is not present where there is not a desire to love him.

LETTER TO THE VENTRELLA SISTERS, DECEMBER 15, 1916

*Y*ou must have boundless faith in the divine goodness, for the victory is absolutely certain. How could you think otherwise? Isn't our God more concerned about our salvation than we are ourselves? Isn't he stronger than hell itself? Who can ever resist and overcome the King of the heavens? What are the world, the devil, the flesh and all our enemies before the Lord?

LETTER TO RAFFAELINA CERASE, APRIL 25, 1914

*Y*our heart is small, but it is expandable, and when it can no longer contain the grandeur of the Beloved, and resist its immense pressure, do not fear, because he is both inside and out; by pouring himself into the interior, he will surround the walls. Like an open shell in the ocean, you will drink your fill and, exuberantly, you will be surrounded and carried along by his power.

LETTER TO GIROLAMA LONGO, JULY 29, 1920

$\mathcal{P}$ERSEVERANCE

*It is always necessary to go forward,
never backward,
in the spiritual life; a boat which stops
instead of going forward,
is blown backward by the wind.*

FOR HISTORY

$\mathcal{I}$ keep my eyes fixed on the East, in the night which surrounds me, to discover that miraculous star which guided our forebears to the grotto of Bethlehem.

LETTER TO PADRE BENEDETTO, MARCH 8, 1916

$\mathcal{S}$ pin a little every day, thread by thread weave your design until it is finished and you will infallibly succeed. But be careful not to hurry, because you will tangle the thread with knots and confuse the spindle. Therefore advance always, and even if you progress at a slow pace, you will still travel far.

LETTER TO THE VENTRELLA SISTERS, OCTOBER 1, 1917

$\mathcal{B}$ e always faithful to God in keeping the promises made to him and do not bother about the ridicule of the foolish. Know that the saints were always sneered at by the world and worldlings; and they have trampled them underfoot and have triumphed over the world and its maxims.

COUNSELS

$\mathcal{D}$o not abstain from doing good due to silly and useless apprehension. If there are foolish people who make fun of the work of the children of God, have a good laugh at them and continue to do the work you started. The divine Master has promised a reward not to those who begin well, but to those who persevere to the end. Let the example of Judas be sufficient for you; who began well, continued to do good, but did not persevere to the end, so [he was] lost.

LETTER TO VIOLANTE MASONE, MAY 19, 1921

$\mathcal{H}$e who attaches himself to the earth, remains attached to it. We are obliged to leave it. It is better to become detached a little at a time, rather than all at once. Let us always think of heaven.

ADVICE AND EXHORTATIONS OF
PADRE PIO OF PIETRELCINA

The children of Israel traveled for 40 years in the desert before setting foot in the Promised Land. Six weeks were more than sufficient to make that journey, but nevertheless they were not permitted to question God's decision to keep them for such a long time in the desert […].

[…] I implore you in the most sweet Lord to pay little attention to the path on which the Lord places you in order to arrive at the Promised Land […]. But rather, I exhort you, by the meekness of Jesus, to keep your eyes always fixed on he who guides you, and on the heavenly Homeland to which he wants to lead you. Why should you worry whether Jesus wants you to reach the Homeland by way of the desert or through fields, when one way or the other you will reach blessed eternity just the same?

LETTER TO THE VENTRELLA SISTERS,
DECEMBER 3, 1916

If you do good, praise and thank the Lord for it; if you happen to sin, humble yourself, propose to do better, ask for help and carry on traveling the right path.

LETTER TO ERMINIA GARGANI, AUGUST 28, 1918

$\mathcal{W}$e must keep the eye of faith fixed on Jesus Christ who climbs the hill of Calvary loaded with his cross, and as he toils painfully up the steep slope of Golgotha we should see him followed by an immense throng of souls carrying their own crosses and treading the same path.

Oh, what a beautiful sight is this! Let us fix our mental gaze firmly on it. We see close behind Jesus our most holy Mother, who follows him perfectly, loaded with her own cross. Then come the apostles, martyrs, doctors, virgins and confessors.

How holy a group, how noble, majestic, estimable and dear to us! Here there is genuine joy, deep peace, courageous progress and a life of perfection! These souls are enlivened by faith, sustained by hope, inflamed with charity, beautified by modesty, adorned by penance.

Here all consolations are combined with every sacrifice, all hope is united with every virtue. Who will grant us to enjoy such marvelous company? But all praise to God! Jesus himself, despite all our unworthiness, has associated us with this beautiful company. We must make every effort to merge ourselves increasingly in these ranks and hasten with them along the road to Calvary. We should look to the end of the journey and not separate ourselves from this fine company; we must refuse to follow any other way than the one they tread.

We must believe that Jesus will invariably sustain us by his grace. We must fight like strong men, with strength of soul, and the prize will not be far off.

LETTER TO PADRE AGOSTINO, JUNE 24, 1915

*W*hat should we say if we were to behold a poor peasant almost stupefied as he continued to gaze at a swiftly flowing river? Perhaps we should just begin to laugh at him and with good reason. Is it not folly to fix our gaze on something that is rapidly passing? This, then, is the state of a person who fixes his eyes on visible things. For what are these things in reality? Are they perhaps different from a swiftly flowing river on whose waters we have no sooner laid eyes than they disappear from our sight, never to be seen again? [...]

Let the consideration of all those good things to be possessed in [paradise] provide us with delightful food for our thoughts. [...O]nly then shall we be able to repeat with full conviction along with the indomitable martyr Saint Ignatius: *Oh, how worthless is the earth, when I look at heaven!*

LETTER TO RAFFAELINA CERASE, OCTOBER 10, 1914

*I*t is difficult to become a saint. Difficult, but not impossible.

The road to perfection is long, as long as one's lifetime.

Along the way, consolation becomes rest; but as soon as your strength is restored, you must diligently get up and resume the trip.

ARCHIVES OF PADRE PIO

*W*hen you are unable to take big steps on the paths to which the Lord leads you, be content with small steps and patiently wait until you have the legs to run, or better still, wings to fly. Be content, my good daughter, with being a little honey bee in a hive for the present; a little bee that will very quickly become a big bee, able to manufacture honey […].

LETTER TO ANNITA RODOTE, AUGUST 16, 1918

$\mathcal{I}$t is necessary, even though you keep going ahead, to diligently apply yourself to face up to the hurdle nearest to you, which it is possible to overcome, and to complete the first day well, without dwelling upon the desire to complete the last, when there is still the first to do. Very often we are so intent upon our desire to become angels in heaven, that we forget to be good Christians. [...I]t is not possible for us to desire and pretend to arrive in only a day [...] and although it is true that we must not rest or turn back, we also must not think to fly, because along the roads of the spirit we are only like little chicks, who have not developed their wings.

PADRE PIO: PASTOR OF SOULS

$\mathcal{O}$h my dearest daughters, this life is short, the rewards for what we achieve in it are eternal. Let us do good, adhere to the will of God; let this be the star on which we rest our gaze during this navigation, because in this way we cannot but reach the heavenly port. Let us not silence our expectations of the holy eternity to which we aspire.

LETTER TO MARIA GARGANI, OCTOBER 4, 1917

$\mathcal{P}$RAYERS AND BLESSINGS

This heart of mine is yours—
my Jesus, take this heart of mine,
fill it with your love, and then do
with me what you will.

DIARY

DIARY

Stay with me, Lord, for it is necessary to have you present so that I do not forget you. You know how easily I abandon you.

Stay with me, Lord, because I am weak, and I need your strength that I may not fall so often.

Stay with me, Lord, for you are my light, and without you I am in darkness.

Stay with me, Lord, to show me your will.

Stay with me, Lord, so that I hear your voice and follow you.

Stay with me, Lord, for I desire to love you very much and to be in your company always.

Stay with me, Lord, if you wish me to be faithful to you.

Stay with me, Lord, for as poor as my soul is I want it to be a place of consolation for you, a nest of love.

Stay with me, Jesus, for it is getting late and the day is coming to a close and life passes—death, judgment, eternity approaches. It is necessary to renew my strength, so that I will not stop along the way and for that, I need you. It is getting late and death approaches. I fear the darkness, the temptations, the dryness, the cross, the sorrows. How I need you, my Jesus, in this night of exile!

Stay with me, Jesus, in life with all its danger, I need you.

Let me recognize you as your disciples did at the breaking of the bread, so that the eucharistic Communion be the light which disperses the darkness, the force that sustains me, the unique joy of my heart.

Stay with me, Lord, because at the hour of my death I want to remain united to you, if not by Communion, then at least by your grace and love.

Stay with me, Jesus. I do not ask for divine consolation because I do not merit it. But the gift of your presence—oh, yes! I ask this of you!

Stay with me, Lord, for it is you alone I look for: your love, your grace, your will, your heart, your spirit, because I love you and ask no other reward but to love you more and more.

With a firm love, I will love you with all my heart while on earth and continue to love you perfectly during all eternity. Amen!

Oh God, the King of my heart, the only source of all my happiness, how much longer must I wait before I can openly enjoy your ineffable beauty? You pierce my heart with the arrows of your love; you are that cruel one who opens deep wounds in my heart although they cannot be perceived; you kill me without taking any care to raise me up again in your own heavenly abode!

What comfort will you offer to this soul which finds no consolation here below and can have no peace while far from you? You are even cruel, Oh my most sweet Creator and my God, to see me languishing for you without being in the least moved, without removing from me the only cause of all this suffering: this life which keeps me far from true life. Oh too long life! Oh cruel life! Oh life that is no longer life to me!

Oh, how lonely I feel, my God and my most tender Savior, in this desert of the world. Can't you see, then, that there is no remedy for my illness? May I hope to be no longer consumed for you?

LETTER TO PADRE AGOSTINO, SEPTEMBER 25, 1915

Oh my dear Jesus…. How can I live without you?…Come often, my Jesus…. You alone can possess my heart…. If I had all the hearts in the world I would offer them to you…. My sweet Jesus, my love for you keeps me going. […]

ECSTASY TRANSCRIBED BY PADRE AGOSTINO
ON DECEMBER 12, 1911

My most pure Mother, my soul so poor, all stained with wretchedness and sin cries out to your maternal heart. In your goodness deign, I beseech you, to pour out on me at least a little of the grace that flowed into you with such infinite profusion from the heart of God. Strengthened and supported by this grace, may I succeed in better loving and serving Almighty God who filled your heart completely, and who created the temple of your body from the moment of your Immaculate Conception.

MEDITATION PRAYER ON MARY IMMACULATE

Oh holy souls free from all anxiety, who are already made happy in heaven by that torrent of supreme sweetness, how I envy you your happiness! Ah, for pity's sake, since you are so close to the Fountain of Life, since you see me dying of thirst in this despicable world, be propitious to me and give me a little of that delightfully fresh water.

LETTER TO PADRE AGOSTINO, OCTOBER 17, 1915

May Jesus be always in your mind, in your heart and before your eyes.

May he invariably be your beginning, your continuation and your end and absorb your entire life into himself.

LETTER TO PADRE AGOSTINO, JULY 10, 1915

$\mathcal{M}$ay Jesus' Mother and ours obtain for us from her Son the grace to live a life entirely according to the heart of God, a completely interior life altogether hidden in him. May this most dear Mother unite us so closely with Jesus that we may never allow ourselves to be enraptured or lured away by anything belonging to this despicable world. May she keep us always close to infinite sweetness, to Jesus.

LETTER TO PADRE AGOSTINO, JULY 10, 1915

$\mathcal{M}$ay Jesus be the star which guides our steps constantly in the wilderness of this present life and bring us without delay to the haven of salvation!

LETTER TO PADRE BENEDETTO, OCTOBER 8, 1920

$\mathcal{M}$ay Mary be the star which shines on your path and may she show you the safe way to reach the heavenly Father. May she be like an anchor to which you must be more closely attached in time of trial.

LETTER TO RAFFAELINA CERASE, MARCH 25, 1915

$\mathcal{I}$ wish you, from the dear Redeemer, the grace of steadfastness of purpose, and especially that of being silent and letting everything around you be silent, in order to hear the voice of the Beloved and establish a peaceful dialogue with him.

LETTER TO MARIA GARGANI, APRIL 28, 1919

$\mathcal{M}$ay your good guardian angel always watch over you; may he be your guide on the bitter paths of life. May he always keep you in the grace of Jesus and sustain you with his hands so that you may not stumble on a stone. May he protect you under his wings from all the snares of the world, the devil and the flesh.

LETTER TO ANNITA RODOTE, JULY 15, 1915

$\mathcal{M}$ay Jesus comfort you in all your afflictions; may he sustain you in dangers, watch over you always with his grace, indicate the safe path that leads to eternal salvation, and may he render you always dearer to his divine heart and always more worthy of paradise.

LETTER TO ERMINIA GARGANI,
NOVEMBER 27, 1920

$\mathcal{M}$ay Jesus, the sun of eternal justice and infinite and immense beauty, always shine in your soul, warming and inflaming it with his holy love and rendering it more and more worthy of him!

LETTER TO ANTONIETTA VONA, MARCH 29, 1919

$\mathcal{M}$ay Jesus always be the supreme King of your heart; may he grant the ardent prayers which he himself places in your heart, and truly fill it with his holy and divine love! Amen.

LETTER TO ANNITA RODOTE, OCTOBER 31, 1915

$\mathcal{M}$ay the peace of Jesus be always in your heart and make you happy.

LETTER TO PADRE AGOSTINO, JUNE 22, 1914

$\mathcal{M}$y soul is full of gratitude to God for the many victories it obtains at every instant, and I cannot refrain from uttering endless hymns of blessing to this great and munificent God. Blessed be the Lord for this great goodness! Blessed be his great mercy! Eternal praise be to such tender and loving compassion!

LETTER TO PADRE AGOSTINO, SEPTEMBER 25, 1915

$\mathcal{B}$less me with a big blessing and recommend me to Jesus, while I continue to do likewise for you.

LETTER TO PADRE BENEDETTO, MAY 27, 1915

ℱINAL THOUGHTS

You must love, love, love above all else.

BETWEEN THE MYSTERIES OF SCIENCE
AND THE LIGHT OF FAITH

*H*ow good Jesus is to us!

LETTER TO PADRE AGOSTINO, SEPTEMBER 1, 1916

*I*t is sufficient for us to know that God is our God, and that our heart is his home.

LETTER TO THE CAMPANILE SISTERS, AUGUST 18, 1918

*N*ever think…that physical distance can separate the souls which God has united with the ties of his love.

PADRE PIO: PASTOR OF SOULS

I belong entirely to everyone. Everyone can say, "Padre Pio is mine." I deeply love [all humanity]. I love my spiritual children as much as my own soul and even more. I have regenerated them to Jesus through suffering and love. I can forget myself but not my spiritual children. Indeed, I can assure you that when the Lord calls me, I will say to him: "Lord, I will stand at the gates of heaven until I see all my spiritual children have entered."

ARCHIVES OF PADRE PIO

PERMISSIONS AND ACKNOWLEDGMENTS

I thank the following people for all their help, without which this book would not have been possible: Judy Bauer, John Cleary, and Cecelia Portlock. My special thanks go out to Rayner W. Hesse, Jr., for his assistance with proofreading, his practical suggestions, his invaluable insights, and, most of all, his sincere interest in my work.

Every effort has been made to locate and secure permission for the inclusion of all copyrighted material in this book. If any such acknowledgments have been inadvertently omitted, the publisher would appreciate receiving full information so that proper credit may be given in future editions.

The compiler wishes to express his gratitude to the following for granting permission to reproduce material of which they are the publisher or copyright holder:

Excerpts from *"Send Me Your Guardian Angel"* by Fr. Alessio Parente, Cap., and *Padre Pio* by Fr. John Schug, Cap., are used with permission of the National Centre for Padre Pio, Inc., Barto, Pennsylvania, U.S.A.

Excerpts from *Advice and Exhortations of Padre Pio of Pietrelcina, Archives of Padre Pio, Diary, For History, Fragments of Light, The Good Shepherd, Padre Pio Answers…, Between the Mysteries of Science and the Light of Faith, San Giovanni Rotondo: In the Light of Franciscanism, Time of Birth, The Time-piece of the Passion of Our Lord Jesus Christ*, as found in *"Have a Good Day"* by Our Lady of Grace Friary, are used with permission of the National Centre for Padre Pio, Inc., Barto, Pennsylvania, U.S.A.

Selections from Padre Pio, *Meditation Prayer on Mary Immaculate*, trans. by Laura Chandler White, Rockford, Ill.: TAN Books and Publishers, 1974, are reprinted with permission.

Selections from Padre Pio, *The Agony of Jesus in the Garden of Gethsemane*, Rockford, Ill.: TAN Books and Publishers, 1974, are reprinted with permission.

OTHER SOURCES

Leone, Gherardo. *Padre Pio and His Work*. San Giovanni Rotondo: Editions Casa Sollievo della Sofferenza, 1986.

Padre Pio. *Counsels*, ed. by P. Alessio Parente. Dublin: Padre Pio Office, 1982.

Padre Pio. *Letters, Volume I: Correspondence with His Spiritual Directors (1910–1922)*, ed. by Melchiorre of Pobladura and Alessandro of Ripabottoni, English version edited by Father Gerardo Di Flumeri, O.F.M.Cap. San Giovanni Rotondo: Our Lady of Grace Capuchin Friary, 1984.

Padre Pio. *Letters, Volume II: Correspondence with Raffaelina Cerase, Noblewoman (1914–1915)*, ed. by Melchiorre of Pobladura and Alessandro of Ripabottoni, English version edited by Father Gerardo Di Flumeri, O.F.M.Cap. San Giovanni Rotondo: Our Lady of Grace Capuchin Friary, 1984.

Padre Pio. *Letters, Volume III: Correspondence with His Spiritual Daughters (1915–1923)*, ed. by Melchiorre of Pobladura and Alessandro of Ripabottoni, Italian version edited by Father Gerardo Di Flumeri, O.F.M.Cap., English version edited by Father Alessio Parente, O.F.M.Cap. San Giovanni Rotondo: Our Lady of Grace Capuchin Friary, 1994.

Padre Pio: Pastor of Souls. San Giovanni Rotondo: Editions Casa Sollievo della Sofferenza, 1992.

Parente, Pascal P. *A City on a Mountain: Padre Pio of Pietrelcina, O.F.M.Cap.* St. Meinrad's Abbey, 1952.

Ruffin, C. Bernard. *Padre Pio: The True Story*. Revised and expanded. Huntington, Ind.: Our Sunday Visitor, 1991.

PHOTO CREDIT

Interior photo: Catholic News Service